Volume Two
For Children Ages 6-9

101 THINGS —TO DO— TO DEVELOP YOUR CHILD'S GIFTS & TALENTS

Developed & Written by
SUSAN AMERIKANER

Illustrated by
TONY GLEASON

Creative Consultant:
Sarina Simon

TOR ®

A TOM DOHERTY ASSOCIATES BOOK

To my husband Erik,
who is a gifted and talented human being;
and to my children Jonathan and Michael,
who take after their dad.

101 THINGS TO DO TO DEVELOP YOUR CHILD'S GIFTS & TALENTS:
VOLUME TWO FOR CHILDREN AGES 6–9

Copyright © 1989 by RGA Publishing Group, Inc. and Susan Amerikaner.

A TOR Book
Published by Tom Doherty Associates, Inc.
49 West 24 Street
New York, NY 10010

Cover art by Doug Fornuff
Book design by Stacey Simons/Neuwirth & Associates

ISBN: 0-812-59392-8   Can. ISBN: 0-812-59393-6

Library of Congress Catalog Card Number: 88-51641

First edition: May 1989

Printed in the United States of America

0 9 8 7 6 5 4 3 2 1

About the Author

Susan Amerikaner specializes in making education fun for children and adults. A native of Baltimore, Maryland, she received her bachelor's degree in creative writing from the University of Maryland and her Master of Arts in Teaching from George Washington University.

As a teacher in Montgomery County, Maryland, Amerikaner taught every elementary grade level and served as school coordinator of activities for gifted and talented students. Mickey Mouse interrupted her teaching career and transplanted Amerikaner to Los Angeles, where she developed a line of classroom materials for the Walt Disney Educational Media Company.

Amerikaner has written several children's books, including *It's O.K. to Say No to Drugs!* She is the creator and author of the *Gifted and Talented Workbook* series.

Currently a writer and consultant for a number of publishers and media companies, Amerikaner resides in Chatsworth, California, with her husband and two sons.

From the Author

Every parent would like to have a gifted child. Many do, but don't know it! Child development experts assert that almost every child has some innate gifts and talents which will flourish—if they are nurtured. This book is designed to help you cultivate your child's natural abilities. These activities are appropriate for children from ages six through nine—*in general*. You are the best judge of whether a particular activity suits your child's level of ability and interest.

While designing a curriculum for gifted elementary school students, I realized that such a curriculum had a much broader application. Gifted education focuses on teaching children *how to think*. What student doesn't need to learn how to think?

I began using the gifted curriculum in all of my classes, and the results were what I expected. Just about every child improved in the areas of critical and creative thinking.

WHY ARE THINKING SKILLS IMPORTANT?

Critical and creative thinking skills are the skills of logic, reasoning, and imagination which enable a child to learn virtually anything. Facts change. Thinking skills do not. A child who knows how to think and reason effectively will be able to approach new tasks with confidence. A child who knows how to think may not know all the answers, but he or she will know how to find them.

Here are some of the key critical and creative thinking skills emphasized in this book:

Sequencing: putting things in order.

Inference: gathering bits and pieces of information and drawing a conclusion.

Deduction: drawing conclusions by using inference and complex clues, including negative clues.

Creativity: creating original ideas; accumulating details; understanding relationships among things that seem dissimilar; applying imagination when solving problems.

HOW YOU CAN HELP

You don't have to be a teacher or a scientist to encourage your child to think. You simply need to be willing to listen and guide, not unlike a travel agent!

Listening is vital. Listen for questions. Teachers often report that the brightest students ask a lot of questions, and questions open the door to discovery. Sometimes adults unwittingly shut this door by responding too quickly and *giving* answers. When your child asks you a question, encourage him or her to try and find the answer independently. Be prepared to encounter a certain amount of mess—self-discovery is a messy business. A child looking for answers may spill, break, tear, or bend things.

When you encourage self-discovery, you may find that you have to admit that you don't always know the answers. Then you can join in the experiment or tag along to the library! A good rule of thumb is: try to answer a question with a question. "How do you think we can find out?" is a valuable response.

HOW TO USE THIS BOOK

Each activity in this book is preceded by a brief introduction that states the overall purpose of the activity and outlines the general skills it is designed to reinforce. These are broad guidelines—feel free to stretch an activity and include any other goals or skills you desire.

You don't have to try variations of an activity right away. If you wait for another time, you will have an entirely new activity.

If your child is tired, bored, or just doesn't want to finish an activity—don't. Be alert. If interest wanes, stop. The directions are deliberately labeled "What You *and* Your Child Do" because I hope that you will participate with your child. These activities are intended to encourage independent thinking, but the fun can be shared! Also, only you know how much help your child will need for each activity.

The activities have been designed for their simplicity as well as effectiveness. For most you won't need to buy anything special; you probably will have everything you need around the house.

A SYMBOL TO LOOK FOR

I know how it feels to spend an hour getting an activity ready, only to find that the activity is over in five minutes. With this in mind I have tried to create activities that require as little preparation as possible. But when preparation is necessary, it can make or break an activity. Therefore, when an activity calls for extra setup, I have designated it with this symbol:

ABOUT RIGHT ANSWERS

When I teach thinking skills, I am not worried about getting the *right* answers. I'm concerned with motivating children to *look for* answers. I try to teach a child to question, to learn by trial and error and self-discovery. I aim to give a child opportunities, not lessons. This book provides you and your child with 101 such opportunities. I hope you try them all!

Susan Amerikaner

1 Yankee Noodle

There are many commercial word games, but none are as economical as this one, which uses a bag of macaroni. This game cultivates basic vocabulary, reading skills, and creative language ability.

WHAT YOU NEED

A bag of alphabet macaroni or alphabet cereal

WHAT YOU AND YOUR CHILD DO

Scoop out a handful of letters from the bag. How many words can you make from the letters?

This game is fun for the entire family. We like to dump the whole bag of macaroni in the middle of the table and see how long it takes us to use up all the letters. You can also divide into two teams. Divide the bag into two piles and see which team uses all of their letters first.

2 Follow-the-Fives

Counting by twos, fives, and tens is a memory exercise that most children enjoy. Here's a quick way to provide practice.

WHAT YOU NEED

Follow-the-dot coloring or activity book
Typewriter correction fluid
Pencil or thin marker
Crayons

1

Use the typewriter correction fluid to erase the numbers on each follow-the-dot page. Replace the numbers, in order, with multiples of two, five, or ten. You might want to erase only a few numbers at a time so you'll be sure to replace them in the right order.

3 | License Plates

Most children and adults love to figure out the messages on personalized license plates. This activity is not only fun, it enhances skills of inference and decoding. Take advantage of travel time by pointing out these metallic mysteries. At home, create your own license plates. It's fun to do, and it develops critical and creative thinking skills in every member of the family.

Scratch paper
Pencil
Drawing paper
Markers or crayons
Scissors

Each person uses paper and pencil to design a personalized license plate. The plate should not be more than eight letters and/or numbers. Try for seven.

Each license plate should reveal something about the person to whom it belongs. Here are a few examples:

Here's an adaptation of this activity that my students love: Think of a fictional or historical character and imagine what his or her license plate would say. Here are some examples:

Jack Sprat—ETNOFAT
Georgie Porgie—LV2KS
Big Bad Wolf—HUFFPUFF
George Washington—USDAD
Rip Van Winkle—ZZZZZZZ

Design the license plate. Draw the character and the car, too. What kind of car would Rapunzel drive? How about Abe Lincoln?

In my classroom we made a guessing game out of this activity. Children take turns holding up their "fantasy plates" and the others try to guess the character that matches the plate.

4 | Secret Codes

Most children love secret codes. When writing or cracking codes, you utilize a wide range of thinking skills that include inference, decoding, generalization, and creative thinking. On this page is a code that beginning readers enjoy.

Paper and pencil

This is called a box code. To figure it out, read the letters from left to right.

Use this code to write messages to each other. Add as many boxes as you need.

If your child isn't interested in codes yet, wait a few months and try again. There are hundreds of different codes, and many excellent books for young people on this subject. Your librarian can help you.

5 Secret Sock

This game is always a winner. Kids love guessing games, and the wonderful thing about this one is that the players never guess how much this game nurtures their skills of inference and concentration, and improves their basic vocabulary.

WHAT YOU NEED

Plastic letters
One clean sock you don't use anymore

WHAT YOU AND YOUR CHILD DO

Choose a word. Place the letters for this word into the sock. (It's best to begin with three-letter words.) Knot the sock above the letters and give it to the other player. He or she must feel the sock and guess which letters are inside. After guessing the letters correctly, the player removes the letters and rearranges them, attempting to spell the secret word.

6 Time Capsule

The ability to gather information and make predictions is a basic thinking skill. In science we begin by predicting the results of our experiments. In literature we imagine what the next chapter has in store. In this activity we summarize our present and predict our future.

Old tickets, souvenirs, photos, etc.

An empty carton

Paper

Pencil

Markers

Tape or other materials with which to seal the carton

Look at old souvenirs, photos, and other family memorabilia. As you reminisce, point out how these items reveal how people lived in the past. Explain that sometimes people put away a collection of things for a long time. Many years later, people look at these things and learn about the past. A collection of items put away for the future is called a *time capsule*.

Prepare a time capsule for your child to open on a future birthday (perhaps a milestone year such as the first year of junior or senior high). You can choose an earlier date, but try to wait for at least one year.

Select ten to twenty objects, such as awards, photographs, toys, letters, ticket stubs, school papers. Before sealing the capsule, fill out a form like the one below. You can change or add to this form in any way you like.

When I open my time capsule on (Date), (Year), I think that:

I will be living _____.

My best friends will be _____.

My favorite subject will be _____.

My favorite foods will be _____.

Seal the box and put it away in a safe place. How will you remember when to open it? Be sure to find a way to mark the date so that the time capsule will not be forgotten indefinitely.

For more information look up time capsules in the encyclopedia; ask a librarian to help.

7 | Icy Challenge

The best science experiments for children are those that provide opportunities for trial and error. This is one that sparks creative problem-solving skills.

One tray of ice cubes
Sink or bucket of warm water
Clock

Place an ice cube in the warm water and guess how long it will take to melt. Time the actual meltdown (usually about fifteen minutes).

Can you find a way to make the ice cubes last an additional five minutes? You are free to use any supplies you have in the house. (Hint: You will have to insulate the ice cube in some way.) If you succeed, can you explain why your method worked?

8 | Is There Life After Fairy Tales?

What if Goldilocks were alive today? Would she be a beautician? Would she run a health food store that specializes in porridge? This type of silly but thought-provoking question brought a great deal of creative fun to my classroom. Because this activity demands a sense of perspective and irony, I recommend it for children eight and up.

WHAT YOU NEED

Imagination
Paper
Crayons or markers

WHAT YOU AND YOUR CHILD DO

Think of a favorite fairy tale or nursery rhyme character. If this character were alive right now, what would he, she, or it be like? Would this character have a job? A house? Draw a picture showing what that character would look like. Be as silly as you want.

9 If the Sock Fits . . .

Here is a classic thinking problem that is always a winner. Try to solve it in your head. The answer is in the back of the book.

WHAT YOU AND YOUR CHILD DO

There are six pairs of unrolled, separated socks in a drawer. Each pair is a different color. One night the electricity goes out and your room is pitch-dark. You need to get a pair of socks, but you can't see the colors. How many socks would you have to take out of the drawer to be sure that you got at least *one* matching pair?

10 Simon Says "Bleep!"

This is a great game for helping children to formulate questions and think deductively. Participants must identify a mystery action by asking questions about it.

WHAT
YOU
AND
YOUR
CHILD
DO

A leader stands up and gives two actions for the others to perform, just as in a regular game of "Simon Says." (The first action could be patting your head; the second, clapping your hands.) The *third* action is the mystery action (perhaps hopping on one foot). The leader does not *do* this action, but instead stops and says, "Simon says, '*Bleep!*'"

The other players ask questions to find out how to "bleep." The leader must be able to answer the questions with "yes" or "no." The best questions are those that narrow down the possibilities. For example, "Do I use my hands to bleep?" "Do I use my head?" "Do I use my legs?" "Do I use both legs?"

The first player to guess how to "bleep" demonstrates the action, and everyone imitates it. Now this person becomes the leader and gives two more actions and a new "bleep."

11 Matchmaker, Matchmaker

Matching things by feel and sight is an excellent way to enhance visual and tactile discrimination.

WHAT YOU NEED

Ruler
Pencil
Cardboard or heavy paper
Scissors
Jar tops or protractor for drawing circles
One paper bag

WHAT YOU AND YOUR CHILD DO

Draw pairs of shapes on the cardboard or heavy paper: two big circles, two smaller circles, two big squares, two small squares, etc.

Cut out the shapes. Separate them into pairs. Take one shape from each pair and put it into the paper bag. Spread the other shapes out on a table.

Close your eyes, take one shape from the bag and hold it behind your back. Holding the shape behind you, find its match on the table.

Some children are a whiz at this and want more of a challenge. If your child is one of these, cut out more shapes of varying sizes. Have a large, medium, small, and extra small of each shape. If the game is too difficult, use pairs of household objects: two spoons, two paper clips, two shoes, etc.

12 Word Geography

Certain old standards remain fresh for each generation. The game of Geography is one. This game is an adaptation which reinforces beginning reading and spelling skills.

The first player says a word. The next player must say a word that starts with the same letter as the *last* letter in the previous word. If the first player says "man," the next player could say "no." The next word could be "octopus," and so on. Keep a children's dictionary nearby.

To make this game harder, use only the names of countries and states.

13 Egg Roll

This activity not only demonstrates the law of inertia; it makes a great magic trick! Teach it to your child and later he or she can stump friends.

Two eggs (as similar in size and shape as possible): one hard-boiled, one raw

Explain that one egg is hard-boiled and one raw. Mix up the eggs as they lay on the table. Even though the eggs are now mixed up, you can tell which is which— and not by breaking them! How can you do it?

Spin each egg. Then touch each one gently and let go right away. The raw egg will keep moving. The hard-boiled egg stops immediately.

The reason for this is one of Newton's laws of physics: An object in motion tends to remain in motion, and an object at rest tends to remain at rest. What does this principle have to do with the eggs? Give your child a chance to think about this before you provide the explanation.

The material inside the hard-boiled egg is solid. When you spin the egg, all of it moves at once. Inside the raw egg, the liquid yolk is floating inside the liquid white part of the egg. When you spin the raw egg, the yolk and white spin more slowly, slowing the motion of the egg. When you stop the raw egg, the yolk and white keep moving for a short time, and the egg continues to rotate.

14 International Marketplace

This is an international detective game that requires no special materials. It cultivates problem-solving skills and heightens multicultural awareness.

Pencil
Paper
Ordinary household goods

Find things in your home that are made in different countries. How many things from different countries can you find? Get the entire family involved and give a prize to the person who finds items from the most countries.

15 Lights, Camera, Action

Few things enhance creative thinking more than dramatic play. It seems that the puppets don't truly come to life without a stage, but you don't have to be a carpenter to make a wonderful puppet theater. This theater hangs in any household doorway.

One spring tension curtain rod (like the kind used as a shower curtain rod)
Measuring tape or yardstick
Piece of fabric
Needle and thread (or safety pins)
Scissors

Measure the width of the doorway. Cut the fabric in a rectangle that is as wide as the doorway. Fold over the top edge, leaving enough space to slide the rod through. Pin or sew the fabric in place.

You can cut a square out of the fabric to use as a stage, or you can just hold puppets above the curtain.

16 | Homespun Pursuit

Everyone seems to enjoy answering trivia questions. This activity tests memory skills and problem-solving ability. If you don't know the answers, you must figure out how to find them.

WHAT YOU NEED

Index cards
Pencil or pen

WHAT YOU AND YOUR CHILD DO

Have each player write ten questions on index cards. Here are the rules: The answers must be found without having to leave the house. Set a time limit for writing questions and finding answers.

Here are some sample questions:

Give out the question cards and start hunting for answers. Make sure no one has his or her own cards. Write the answers on the back of the cards. All players meet at the agreed upon time to review the answers. The player with the most correct answers wins.

Tic-Tac-Dozen

This tic-tac-toe variation reinforces basic skills while calling for quite a bit of strategy.

Paper
Two crayons,
each a different color

Draw a tic-tac-toe grid. The first player writes a number from one to nine in a square. The second player (using a different color crayon or pencil) writes another number from one to nine in another square. The game continues until one player has written three numbers across, down, or diagonally that total exactly *twelve*. You may use each number more than one time. To make the game more difficult, do not allow a number to be used more than once!

Collections, Not Clutter

When you encourage your child to be a collector, you are cultivating the following skills: classification and sorting, observation, evaluation, inference, and organization.

Notebooks, boxes, or other suitable containers

If your child doesn't know what he or she wants to collect, review our list of suggestions. Flat items can be stored in notebooks. Larger items can be stored in boxes, egg cartons, or similar containers. Take off the tops so that the collections can be displayed, but save the tops for storing the collections later.

It is important to devise a system for marking each item. Include the date and location that each item was acquired. If your collection is kept in a notebook, label each entry. Number bulkier items and keep a corresponding list in a notebook.

Suggestions for Collectibles

bugs	baskets	leaves	pencils
buttons	coins	maps	rocks
buttons or pins with slogans or pictures	toy cars	menus	records
	playing cards	old photographs	rulers
	dolls		stamps
butterflies	greeting cards	postcards	shells
bubble pipes		pens	tickets

19 Good Relations

This sophisticated game is as challenging for adults as for young people. It is an excellent way to practice creative thinking—and creative thinking *can* be practiced! In this exercise you flex your mental muscles with original thinking.

WHAT YOU AND YOUR CHILD DO

The first player says a word or phrase. The next player must devise a word or phrase that is in some way related to the previous word. Play continues with each person giving another word or phrase. The game goes on until a player can't find a way to add one more "relative" to the chain.

Here is an example: baby, diaper, wet, rain, cloud, dark, afraid, monster, Godzilla, King Kong, Tyrannosaurus Rex, meat eater, juicy steak . . .

20 The Write Track

Letter writing is one of the best vehicles for cultivating written communication skills. Provide as many opportunities for letter writing as possible. Don't worry about perfection. Offer spelling and grammar help *only if asked*. Let your child discover the power of the pen.

WHAT YOU NEED

Pens and paper

Write a letter to a favorite author or a celebrity. Your child may receive only a form reply or photograph, but sometimes he or she will receive a personal reply.

Local papers are hungry for timely letters to the editor. Focus on an issue on which your child or your family has an opinion. It doesn't have to be a national issue; a dispute over the building of a shopping center or a proposed switch to year-round schools are excellent topics. Look over other letters to the editor. Make sure that your child uses the correct form and includes his or her name, address, and phone number.

Have you ever purchased a toy or game that didn't live up to its advertising? Most manufacturers have departments of consumer affairs and give serious consideration to such letters. Your child is likely to receive a personal reply.

21 | Listen, My Children

Good listeners are not just born; listening skills can be refined and practiced just like any other. Are adults better listeners than children? I challenge anyone to try the following math problems. The last one is especially tough; the answer is at the end of the book.

These math problems are very easy, *if* you pay attention. Try to figure them out without pencil and paper.

Mary had twenty-five pretzels and ate all but three. How many did she have left?

If you took six cookies from a jar containing twenty cookies, how many cookies would you have?

17

Which weighs more: a pound of rocks or a pound of feathers?

Pretend that you are the owner of a gift shop. In the early morning fifteen people come in and ten buy things. In midmorning twelve people come in, but only six buy gifts. Later sixteen people come in and twelve buy things. Just before closing, three people come in, but they don't buy anything. Does the owner of the shop have blond hair?

Story Box

This activity was a big hit in my classrooms from kindergarten through sixth grade. It stimulates creative thinking, inference, and laughter!

WHAT YOU NEED

Large box or carton
Assortment of objects
Scarf, or something to use as a blindfold
An egg timer

WHAT YOU AND YOUR CHILD DO

Fill the box with as many objects as you can, using only one of each object. Blindfold the first player. He or she reaches into the box to retrieve an object, removes the blindfold, and begins a story based on that object. Each storyteller speaks for two minutes. Then the next player is blindfolded, picks an object from the box and continues the story, adding the new object to the storyline.

It is fun to decorate the box so that it looks like a giant present or surprise box.

23 Cartoon Balloons

Cartoons are wonderful tools for developing skills of inference, sequencing, and creative thinking.

Cartoons from the newspaper
Plain white paper
Paste or glue
Scissors
Large sheet of paper
Pencil

Cut out cartoon strips or single cartoons. Don't limit yourself to the funnies; political or editorial cartoons are perfectly acceptable. Cover the captions or dialogue with plain white paper. Create funny dialogue or captions of your own.

Cartoons are a sophisticated combination of art and words. Dialogue bubbles appear in a variety of shapes that give clues to the meanings of the words within. Exclamations are often contained in pointed balloons. Silent thought is indicated by small, cloudlike bubbles. Look for other symbols. How does the artist indicate a conversation between two or more characters? How do we know if a character is worried? In love? In a hurry? Encourage your child to make his or her own comic creations using these symbolic elements.

Word Discovery

This game fills moments in a waiting room or restaurant while it fills the brain with vocabulary skills. It is a classic word game.

Paper and pencil

INTELLIGENT:
1. Tell   11. Tin
2. Let   12. Till
3. Lit   13. Line
4. Lint   14.
5.   15.
...eg   16.
...nt   17.
...ile   18.
...ine   19.
10. Lilt   20.

Write a long word on the top of a piece of paper. Make as many words as you can using the letters in that word. Some good starting words are: intelligent, extemporaneous, administration, hospitable.

A Picture's Worth at Least One Word

This is a classroom activity that works equally well at home. It is excellent for enhancing creative thinking along with basic vocabulary skills. It does, however, require a certain amount of language sophistication. If your child doesn't seem to get the idea, wait and try again at a later date.

Paper
Markers or crayons

Choose a few words that can be drawn to look like what they mean. Some good words to use are: hair, zoo, bump, cloud, hill, shiver, tall, short, happy, thin, rope, train, snake, jump, pie, wave, and circle. Here are some examples:

26 Paper Clip Trick

Magnets are wonderful tools for hands-on exploration. Keep a supply of inexpensive ones and let your child use them to play, build, and discover.

One magnet
Assorted items (string, scissors, tape, paper, can opener, screwdriver, etc.)
Glass of water
One paper clip

Place the paper clip in the glass of water. It will sink to the bottom. Spread the assorted items (including the magnet) on the table.

Challenge your child to remove the paper clip from the glass of water *without* putting anything into the water or pouring any water out.

The solution is to hold the magnet beneath the glass and then slide the paper clip up the side and out.

27 Lexicogaphy

Here is another activity that stretches creative thinking and basic vocabulary skills. It also requires a change in perspective or point of view. Knowing how to look at something from different angles is an important part of creative problem-solving.

WHAT YOU NEED

Paper and pencil

WHAT YOU AND YOUR CHILD DO

People write dictionaries, so naturally the pages are filled with words that are important to people. Imagine a dictionary written by something non-human!

Write a dictionary of ten to fifteen words as defined by an animal, a character from a favorite story, a plant, or a being on another planet.

28 Dear Captain Hook

One Valentine's Day a local radio station sponsored prizes for the most original valentines. My third and fourth graders wrote valentines in the personas of famous characters. The results were so good that we not only won the prizes, we read the valentines on the air. This activity has become a favorite of mine. I use it with all ages and find that it never fails to inspire writing that is thoughtful, original, and sometimes hilarious! Don't wait until Valentine's Day. This is fun all year.

Paper and pencil

Dear Capt. Hook,
I would love to have you for lunch?
Yours Truly,
Cyrus Q. Crocodile

Think of a famous person or fictional character. Now ask these questions:

"Who would this person write a letter to?"

"What would he or she or it say in this letter?"

Write the letter and, if desired, draw a picture of the people or characters involved.

29 Round and Round

Life is a roller coaster in more ways than one. Use this outdoor experiment to introduce your child to centrifugal force.

One bucket
Water

Fill the bucket half full with water. Ask: What will happen if you swing the bucket around? Move your arms and spin the bucket in a circle—fast! What happens?

The water is held inside the bucket by centrifugal force, which is strong enough to overcome the pull of gravity. Do you know of any amusement park rides that depend on centrifugal force? Why doesn't this experiment work if you move the bucket too slowly?

30 Acrostic Fun

An acrostic sounds like a dry kind of toast, but in the activity below it becomes a wonderful and easy way to enhance vocabulary, creative thinking skills, and self-concept.

Pencil
Paper
Crayons or markers

Make an acrostic out of your name using words that say something special and good about you! Here's an example:

C - Creative
A - Always on time
R - Reasonable
L - Loves Soccer

31 Reversibles

Words that read the same when they are reversed are known as *palindromes* (mom, pop, tot, eye). Numbers can also be palindromes.

Pencil and paper

Write down any number from one to 1,000. Turn this number around so it is reversed. Add this reversed number to the original number. Take the new sum and reverse it. Add the reversed number to the previous number. Keep going until you end up with a "reversible" number. Here is an example:

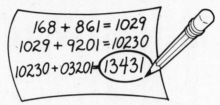

168 + 861 = 1029
1029 + 9201 = 10230
10230 + 03201 = 13431

13431 reads the same backward and forward.

32 Body Suits

This activity does not guarantee that your child will go to medical school, but it does offer an opportunity for informal inquiry and fun.

One plain white T-shirt

Fabric markers

Science or reference book with simple diagrams of internal human organs

Index cards

Crayon

Safety pins

Research and find the location of two to five internal organs. (The heart, lungs, stomach, kidneys, and intestines are all good choices.) Write the name of each organ on an index card. Use a safety pin to affix each card to the T-shirt in the appropriate location. Check each location carefully.

One at a time, remove each index card and use the fabric marker to draw the appropriate organ (directly on the shirt). Now you have an "anatomy T-shirt."

33 Instant Words

Here is a game that reinforces vocabulary skills and instills a respect for the power of vowels!

WHAT YOU NEED

Paper and pencil

WHAT YOU AND YOUR CHILD DO

Take the following words and change them into new words by substituting a new vowel in each one: smell, lick, warm, just, part, hall, block, lamp, top, deer, doll, lend, far, both, crash, stamp, lock, spit, dish.

What's My Category?

Knowing how to classify and categorize is a skill we use constantly. Your brain is like a filing cabinet. If it's messy, you won't be able to find anything. If you label things, you can find the information when you need it.

WHAT YOU NEED

Paper and pencil
Ruler
Twenty-five index cards

WHAT YOU AND YOUR CHILD DO

Write one letter of the alphabet, excluding X, on each index card. Shuffle the cards and place them face down on the table.

Draw a grid as pictured below. Choose five categories and write them in the spaces as pictured. Make the same grid for each player. Here are some suggestions for categories, but the possibilities are infinite: book titles, celebrities, nouns, verbs, street names, cities, countries, things made of wood, metal objects, plastic objects, birds, animals, desserts, drinks, tools, fairy tale characters, fruits, cold foods, hot foods, clothes, insects, presidents, song titles.

Pick five index cards and write the letters in the letter spaces. Each player copies the same letters. You may set a time limit to fill in the grid. Use any reference materials in the house. Players get a point for each correct word. If any players use the same words, no one gets points for it!

CATEGORIES

LETTERS		BIRDS	FOOD	SONGS	GIRLS' NAMES	CITIES
	S		Sandwich			
	T				Tess	
	P					Portland
	R	Robin				
	E					

35 Fat Ice

This is a simple and clear demonstration that is certain to impress your child. Once you witness this, it is difficult to forget that water expands when it is frozen.

WHAT YOU NEED

One jar
One plastic bag large enough to hold the jar with some extra room
Water

WHAT YOU AND YOUR CHILD DO

Fill the jar with water and close the top tightly. Make sure the jar is filled to the very top. Hypothesize what will happen when you put this in the freezer overnight.

Put the jar inside the plastic bag and tie it or close it with a "twisty." Place the bag and jar in the freezer overnight. If it's cold enough, you can put it outside.

What happens? Because water expands when it freezes, the jar should crack. Ask the following questions:

"Why do roads get potholes during the winter?"

"Why isn't it a good idea to leave soda pop outside in the winter?"

"Why would a water pipe burst during the winter?"

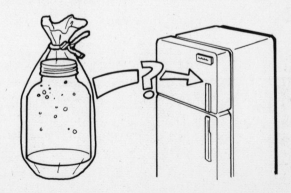

Wizard of AZ

This is a simple game that stimulates creative thinking and is great fun when you're waiting at a restaurant. My children named it the Wizard of AZ game.

Pick a person, place, or object. The first player begins to describe this person, place, or object by starting with the letter A. "Marvin is adorable." The next player goes on with the letter B and so on. Can you describe Marvin from A to Z?

Anagrams

Some people do better with word games on paper. Here is an easy one that is good for beginning readers and writers.

Paper and pencil

Write one letter on the paper. The letter **T** is a good starter. The next player adds one more letter (either before or after the first one) to make a two-letter word.

The next player adds another letter to make a three-letter word. Players can rearrange the letters. Keep going until no more new words can be formed.

26 Skiddoo

This kept my classroom of third and fourth graders busy for most of the afternoon. Even children who hated creative writing had fun with it.

Paper and pencil

Write this sentence: "The quick brown fox jumps over the lazy dog." When people are learning to type, they often practice by typing this sentence again and again. Can you figure out why? (The sentence uses every letter of the alphabet.)

Write a sentence that uses all the letters of the alphabet. What is the shortest one you can write? Anything less than fifty letters is excellent.

Egg Float

Here's another egg-citing experiment that provides an opportunity for inquiry and research. It is another activity that you can stage first. Your child can perform it later to amaze others!

WHAT YOU NEED

Two empty jars
Two pints of water
Eight tablespoons of salt
Two eggs
Spoon

WHAT YOU AND YOUR CHILD DO

Do these two steps where your child cannot see you: Put one pint of tap water in each jar. Add the salt to *one* jar and mix thoroughly. Allow the salt to settle until the water looks clear.

Now get two eggs and put one egg in each jar. One sinks. One floats. Why? (The salt in the water allows the egg to float.)

Once the truth is out, help your child research and find out *why* salty water behaves this way. What would happen if you added sugar to the water? Flour? Food coloring? Anything else? Enjoy experimenting.

My children love performing the "Egg Float" as a magic trick. They ceremoniously chant magic words and bewitch the egg that they know will float!

40 Alphabet Hunt

This is another game that is wonderful for passing the time when you have to wait. It reinforces vocabulary skills and creative thinking.

Paper and pencil

Write the alphabet vertically along the left-hand side of the paper. Look around and write down the name of something in the room that begins with each letter. It's fun to try this game as a family and have everyone contribute to the list.

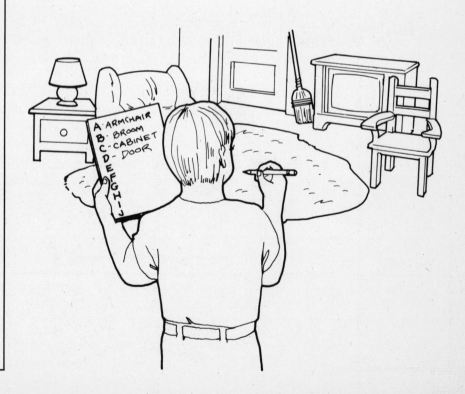

41 Stink Pinks

In many resource books these funny definitions are called Hink Pinks, but my kids always call them Stink Pinks.

Pencil and paper (optional)

A Stink Pink is a set of rhyming words that describe something. Each word in a Stink Pink has one syllable. Here are some Stink Pinks:

> a lot of hair—big wig
>
> an empty seat—bare chair
>
> heated place—hot spot

Here are some Stinky Pinkys (Two Syllables):

> a tired flower—lazy daisy
>
> comical rabbit—funny bunny

One player thinks of a Stink Pink and gives clues to the other players. The player who guesses the correct answer must come up with a new Stink Pink and new clues.

Suggest that your child draw some of the Stink Pinks.

A lot of hair: BIG WIG

An empty seat: BARE CHAIR

A tired flower: LAZY DAISY

Comical rabbit: FUNNY BUNNY

42 What Made It Tick?

Scientists and inventors often reminisce about a childhood in which they were free to explore. Give your child the freedom to take things apart—and learn. Clear a space in a closet, garage, or basement for some old appliances. These can be used as described below, with your close supervision.

WHAT YOU NEED

Old, broken appliance (television, iron, mixer, radio, etc.)
Tools (screwdrivers, wrenches, hammers, etc.)

WHAT YOU AND YOUR CHILD DO

Designate a work area. Spread out an old sheet or newspapers. Open up the appliance and take it apart using the tools. You don't have to be a mechanical genius! Use a do-it-yourself manual or fix-it book to guide you.

43 Taffy Words

This activity stimulates creativity in both children and adults. I call it taffy words because you have to stretch words and ideas until they are flexible enough to meet.

Pencil and paper

Write two words separated by three blanks:

candy _____ _____ _____ hot

Fill in the blanks so that each word has some relationship with the word before and the word after.

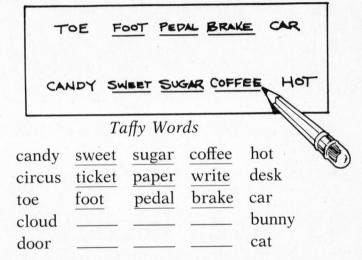

Taffy Words

candy	sweet	sugar	coffee	hot
circus	ticket	paper	write	desk
toe	foot	pedal	brake	car
cloud	_____	_____	_____	bunny
door	_____	_____	_____	cat

This is a fascinating activity. Make sure that you write your first and last words *first*! Don't bother trying to see if they will work—almost any two words can be "pulled" together. It just takes a little ingenuity. This makes a great team game. One team can make up a list of first words, and the other player or team makes up the final words.

44 Storygrams

This is a unique activity in which you transform a well-known fairy tale, poem, story, document, or event into a brief "storygram." Creative thinking skills (fluency, flexibility, and originality) are stimulated by this activity. Laughter is usually stimulated, too!

Pencil and paper

Think of a famous fairy tale, nursery rhyme, story, or poem. Condense it into a ten- to fifteen-word story-gram. An example is below:

45 | Leap Puzzle

This is a particularly good activity for strengthening the skill of inference.

Paper and pencil
Reference books (optional)

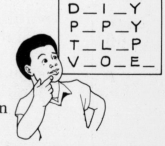

The first player chooses a category, such as flowers. Make a list of five to ten items in the category, skipping every other letter.

The next player fills in the missing letters, using reference books if necessary. Take turns creating puzzles and filling them in.

46 Magic Balloons

Chemistry can begin in the kitchen. The following experiment is easy—and you probably already have everything you need.

WHAT YOU NEED

One funnel

Two teaspoons of baking soda

One small empty soda bottle (I've also used an empty ketchup bottle.)

1/3 cup vinegar

One balloon

WHAT YOU AND YOUR CHILD DO

You are going to mix the vinegar and the baking soda in the bottom of the bottle and then put the balloon on top. What do you think will happen?

Make sure that the bottle is clean and dry inside. Pour the baking soda into the bottle.

Use the funnel to pour the vinegar into the balloon. Fit the neck of the balloon over the neck of the bottle and pull it down to make a tight fit.

Push the balloon up until all the vinegar falls into the bottle, being sure to hold the neck of the balloon tightly. Watch what happens! The vinegar and baking soda have combined to form carbon dioxide.

What would happen if you mixed the baking soda with water and a little soap powder? Some people drink baking soda and water when they have an upset stomach. It usually makes them burp. Why?

47 | Backward Flip

Here's another word game for children who like to be challenged. Keep a dictionary nearby.

Paper and pencil

Think of ten or more words that spell *new* words when their letters are *reversed*. Here are some examples: net, not, gum, lap, pot, on, wed, mar, trap, warts, smart, devil, reward, repaid, step, stab, stun, leek, spar, may, edit, dog, raw, pals, tap, tip, keep, lever, tinker, stinker, sag, nap, star, nip, tool, draw, deer, golf.

48 | Word Vine

This is a classic word building game. It fosters basic vocabulary skills, creativity, and inference.

Pencil and paper

The first player writes a four-letter word at the top of a sheet of paper. The next player changes one letter to make a new word and writes that word beneath the first. The second player continues in this way, changing one letter at a time to make a new word, until he or she can go no further.

You can also play by alternating turns or by working simultaneously, trying to see who can build the longest "vine" in a given amount of time. Here is a sample word vine:

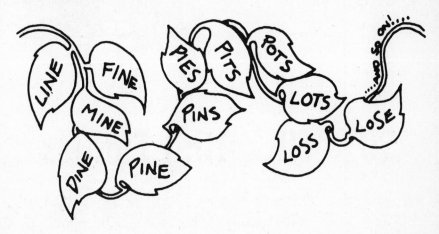

49 | Code-Making With Sound

Decoding is one of the best ways to sharpen inductive and deductive thinking skills. Creating codes is equally effective. Here is a noisy and fun encoding and decoding idea.

Tape recorder and microphone

Blank cassette tape

Pencil and paper

Two people

Write down the alphabet. Think up a sound to match each letter. List the sounds next to the appropriate letters. (A: clap hands; B: cough once; C: bang a pot with a spoon once; etc.) Write a message and use the sound code to record the message on tape. Keep the message simple! Take turns sending and receiving messages.

50 Flickering Flames

This is a classroom favorite, and a demonstration that is easy to duplicate at home. Adult supervision is a must.

Three candles (all the same size)
Three candle holders (If you use those short, squat candles you won't need holders.)
Three jars of different sizes: pint, quart, gallon
Match

Light each candle quickly. Have another adult help if possible, since the candles should be lit at the same time! Place one jar over each candle. Ask: What is inside an empty jar? (Oxygen)

Can your child guess which candle will go out first, second, and third? Time what really happens. Discuss the results. Why did the candle under the smallest jar go out more quickly? (Fire needs oxygen to burn. The candle whose jar held the most oxygen should have burned the longest.)

51

Who's in the Club?

This activity encourages a child to search for subtle similarities and to formulate and test hypotheses.

WHAT YOU NEED

Pictures of ten or more people, either snapshots or clippings from magazines

WHAT YOU AND YOUR CHILD DO

Spread the pictures out on a table. Silently choose a characteristic that two or more of the people in the pictures have in common: long hair, casual clothes, tall, thin, happy, winter clothes.

Announce to your child that some of the people in the pictures are in a secret club because they have one special thing in common. Your child should try to guess who is in the club by asking questions to which you can answer "yes" or "no."

Most children begin by pointing to certain pictures and asking, "Is he in the club?" "Is she in the club?" After several members of the club are identified, your child can begin to guess which *characteristic* makes them a member.

To make this game more difficult, select *two* characteristics: blue eyes and white socks, curly hair and a belt.

Bookworm Code

In the classroom I used outdated grammar books and readers for this activity. At home it works well with magazines or newspapers.

Two copies of the same book, magazine, or newspaper

Pencil and paper

In this simple code each number stands for the page, line, and word in a certain book. Here is a sample: 14-26-4 would mean page 14, line 26, word 4. If there are columns on the page, add another number in the second position: 4-2-12-5 for page 4, column 2, line 12, word 4.

Sour Notes

My sons love writing messages with invisible ink—and reading them! This activity combines reading, language, problem-solving skills, and chemistry. Please note that heat is needed to read the messages—so adult supervision is necessary!

One lemon or grapefruit

One shallow dish

Plastic toothpick or fine brush

Plain white paper

Lamp

Squeeze the lemon or grapefruit juice into the dish. Dip the brush or toothpick into the juice and write a message on the paper. When the ink dries, it disappears. To read the message, you must warm up the paper by holding it up to a light bulb or ironing it with an iron set on low heat.

What makes the ink invisible? The juice contains carbon compounds which are colorless until they are heated. Ask your child to think about what happens when you burn toast: it is a similar chemical reaction.

Several other household ingredients work well as invisible inks:

> Dissolve a few teaspoons of sugar in a cup of warm water.
>
> Use a carbonated drink, such as orange soda pop.
>
> Mix some strawberry jam with a little water.
>
> Dissolve one teaspoon of salt in warm water. Cool.

54 Detective Eyes

In this exercise the participants must rely on keen powers of observation as well as visual memory.

Face each other. Tell your child to look at you very, very carefully. Explain that after a few minutes you are going to leave the room, change one thing about yourself (tuck in a shirt, open a button, move a belt, etc.), and return. Your child will have to point out what is different about you. Take turns being the observer and the "changer."

55 Handy Notes

Most children do not use formal note-taking in school until the upper elementary or junior high level. However, there are plenty of opportunities for children to develop good note-taking habits much earlier. They are often asked to watch a video tape or movie and remember salient facts. Here is a simple but valuable hint which gives youngsters a running start.

Pen or pencil
Paper

Here's the hint: Do *not* hold your pen or pencil when you take notes! When you hold a pen or pencil, you become easily distracted. You doodle. You tap. You might even chew on the pencil or eraser. All these minor distractions take away from the real job—listening. Not holding the pen forces you to listen.

When *do* you pick up your pen or pencil to set down a few key words? Only when you understand the subject! If you waste time listing questions about things you don't understand, you might miss the explanation. Write down your questions at the end, after you have heard everything.

This technique takes some getting used to, especially in adults, who have established habits. Try it as a family! Watch a television show in which important information will be given and use this method of note-taking. You will be surprised at how much more effective your notes will be and how much more you will remember.

56 Fossil Fun

Most children are fascinated with fossils. It's not too hard to make homemade fossils.

Plaster of Paris (available at a hobby store)
Plastic container
Petroleum jelly
One shell, leaf, twig, chicken bone, or any other object
Water

Prepare plaster according to the directions. Fill the plastic container with plaster. Coat the object with petroleum jelly. Wait until the plaster is almost set and place the object on the plaster. Press gently, so that the object presses into the plaster but is not buried in it. Wait twenty minutes, until the plaster is hard. Remove the object.

How is this process similar to the real process by which fossils are formed? How is it different?

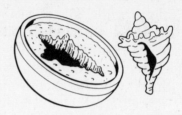

57 | Alphabet Clues

This is a language game that develops skills in deductive reasoning and descriptive language.

Twenty-four index cards
Marker

Mark each index card with a letter of alphabet, excluding X and Z. Shuffle the cards and place them face down in a pile. Choose a card. Make up a question about an object that begins with that letter. For example, if you turn up a **B,** you could ask, "What starts with **B** and flies?"

Your partner tries to answer. The answer is correct as long as it makes sense and starts with the correct letter. In the example above, either "bird" or "butterfly" would be correct.

If the answer is correct, the guesser keeps the card. If the answer is wrong, the card is placed at the bottom of the deck. Take turns drawing cards and asking questions. The game stops when all the cards are gone, and the winner is the person with the most cards.

58 Homemade Twisters

My children think tongue twisters are hilarious. But they like them even more when they create their own. I wouldn't dare tell them how much good it does for their creativity and vocabulary skills.

WHAT YOU NEED

Paper and pencil

WHAT YOU AND YOUR CHILD DO

Review a few well-known tongue twisters (Peter Piper; She sells seashells . . .). Now make up some of your own. It's easier if you use a pattern:

Adjective—Name—Verb—When, Where or What happened

Example: Mealy-mouthed Marvin made mud Monday morning.

Suggest that your child illustrate the tongue twisters he or she has created.

59 Introduction to Physics

Several laws of physics lend themselves to surprisingly simple home demonstrations. These demonstrations should lead to more inquiry and stir thinking skills.

WHAT YOU NEED

A few straight drinking straws
A few long balloons
Masking tape
Nylon thread
Two kitchen chairs
Ruler
Scissors
Reference books with pictures of and information about jet planes

WHAT YOU AND YOUR CHILD DO

Explain that long ago the famous scientist Sir Isaac Newton proved that when force is applied in one direction, there is equal force in the opposite direction. This is not hard to understand, and you can use a balloon and a straw to demonstrate!

Set the two chairs ten to twelve feet apart. Tie the thread to one chair, pass it through the straw, and tie it to the other chair. Pull the thread taut.

Cut about four inches of tape and place it over the middle of the straw so that the ends of the tape hang down on each side. Blow up the balloon. Don't let the air out of the balloon, but don't tie a knot—hold the balloon closed with your fingers.

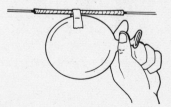
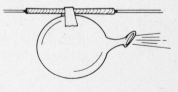

Attach the balloon to the two overlapping pieces of tape, as close to the middle of the balloon as possible.

Slide the balloon and the straw to one end of the string, with the neck of the balloon nearest the chair. Let go! What happens? How does this demonstrate the law that force in one direction is equal to force in the opposite direction? (The air in the balloon went backward pushing the straw forward.) Try it again.

What does this experiment have to do with the way a jet flies? (A jet engine burns compressed gases which are thrown or thrust backward, much like the air inside the balloon. This backward thrust propels the plane forward.)

60 | My Own Fables

Any parent interested in enriching a child should not fail to read aloud a selection of Aesop's Fables. Once your child has a feel for Aesop's stories, he or she can create original fables.

Paper and pencil
Crayons or markers

Read several morals or proverbs, one at a time. Discuss what they mean. Be sure to listen to your child's explanation!

Choose one moral or proverb and write or tell a story that demonstrates this moral. You may want to write and illustrate several of these stories and put them in a book. Here are some well-known morals to get you started:

A fool and his money are soon parted.

All that glitters is not gold.

Sometimes silence is the best reply.

The guilty conscience needs no accuser.

A bird in the hand is worth two in the bush.

Even when he tells the truth, a liar is not believed.

61 | Because—Why—Because

This game builds creativity and logic skills at the same time.

**WHAT
YOU
AND
YOUR
CHILD
DO**

The first person makes a logical cause and effect statement: "I missed the bus because I got up late."

The next person takes the last part of that sentence and makes it the first part of a new cause and effect statement: "I got up late because my alarm did not go off."

This continues until someone makes a statement that is not logical or cannot think of a new cause and effect sentence to continue the story.

62 Magnetic Monsters

It is not a surprise to find that children learn when they have fun. Here is a guaranteed good time with magnets.

WHAT YOU NEED

A good magnet
Clay or play dough
A few thumbtacks
A paper plate

WHAT YOU AND YOUR CHILD DO

Use the clay or play dough to make a small figure of a monster or an animal. Put one or two thumbtacks (close together) in the bottom of the monster. Sit the monster on the paper plate. Hold your magnet under the plate and move your monster around. It's fun to give a magnetic puppet show this way!

63 Ding-Dong-Ding

In this language game the participants practice classification, listening, and vocabulary skills. They also have a lot of fun.

WHAT YOU NEED

Paper
and pencil

Fold the paper in half vertically, or draw a line down the middle. On the left top half write *Ding*. On the right: *Ding-Dong*.

Underneath *Ding*, write the name of a category. Underneath *Ding-Dong*, write the name of another category. One player begins naming things. After each word, the other player says "Ding" or "Ding-Dong," depending on the correct category for each word. If the word doesn't fit either category, the player must remain silent.

Play continues until the second player misses. Then he or she gets a turn to make up categories and you get to Ding-Dong!

64 Inventive Thinking

Invention is the process of creativity put to practical use. Although it seems as though we have just about everything we could ever need, each age brings new inventions. Once my class of second graders was intrigued by a newspaper article which reported on the silent, unfriendly way most people ride together on elevators. The children were inspired to draw pictures of their own inventions that would alleviate this sad situation. Some were silly, some were profound, but they were all published in the Sunday supplement!

Paper and pencil

Dream up an invention that would make life better, easier, or happier. Illustrate and name your invention.

The Friendly Elevator Machine is a good example. Here are some more suggestions, but the best inventions are those that come from your own needs. Invent something that will . . .

> stop all traffic jams
>
> get everyone to the breakfast table at the same time
>
> make your bed
>
> get you dressed while you're still asleep
>
> clean the house
>
> exercise and do homework at the same time
>
> let you eat without ever getting fat

Give the finished invention a name, and draw a picture of it.

Treasure Hunt

Once a child is a fluent reader, a treasure hunt becomes irresistible. It is a great way to nurture deductive reasoning skills.

Notepaper
Envelopes
Pen or pencil
A prize (a healthy
snack, a new book, etc.)

Hide the prize somewhere in the house. Write a series of clues on individual pieces of notepaper. "Look under the sofa." "Try behind the piano."

Seal each clue in an envelope and place them in the appropriate places. Include some negative clues, such as: "The next clue is near the blue chair, but it is not under the chair." The other players open and read each clue until the prize is found.

No Repeats

A deck of cards is one of the best educational tools you can buy. In this tough game you work on inference, memory, and problem-solving skills.

All the picture cards from one deck of cards and the aces

Arrange the cards in four rows of four cards each—so that no row across, down, or corner-to-corner diagonally has two cards of the same suit or rank. The solution is in the back of this book.

67 Fantasy Recipes

This is another successful classroom technique for promoting creative thinking. It works well for a group or for an individual child.

Pencil and paper
Crayons or markers

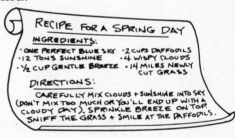

RECIPE FOR A SPRING DAY
INGREDIENTS:
• ONE PERFECT BLUE SKY • 2 CUPS DAFFODILS
• 12 TONS SUNSHINE • 4 WISPY CLOUDS
• ½ CUP GENTLE BREEZE • 14 MILES NEWLY
                            CUT GRASS
DIRECTIONS:
CAREFULLY MIX CLOUDS + SUNSHINE INTO SKY
(DON'T MIX TOO MUCH OR YOU'LL END UP WITH A
CLOUDY DAY). SPRINKLE BREEZE ON TOP.
SNIFF THE GRASS + SMILE AT THE DAFFODILS.

Review the two segments of any food recipe: the *ingredients* and the *directions*. It might help to look at a few cookbooks.

Your child's job is to create a recipe for something that *cannot be eaten*. How would he or she write a recipe for a spring day, a birthday party, a hug, a rainstorm, or a rainbow?

Once your child has invented the recipe, encourage him or her to write it down and illustrate it.

Spell-Out

Even gifted children need to study spelling lists! Here is a way to make spelling practice fun.

Words to spell
Pencil and paper

Write these letters: a, e, i, o, u, l, n, r, s, and t. These are the most frequently used letters. Most of them are likely to appear on your child's spelling list.

Make up an action to stand for each of these letters. Jot down a brief description of the action next to each letter (a: clap your hands; e: touch your nose; i: point to your eyes; etc.).

Your child can use these actions to practice spelling words. It's much more fun if you join in, too.

The Case of the Missing Letter

Here is another excellent activity that reinforces basic phonics and vocabulary along with deductive thinking.

Index cards
Pen or marker

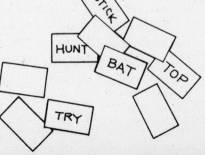

On each index card write a one-syllable word that your child can read. Spread the cards face up on the table. Give your child a few minutes to read them all.

Ask your child to leave the room or turn away. Pick one letter that two or more words have in common. Turn all the word cards that include this letter face down. Can your child figure out which letter is missing? Try taking turns with this game.

70 More Tricky Thinking

Here are more classic thinking problems. They challenge you and your child to think critically and creatively. Take the challenge before you turn to the back for answers.

Answer these brainteasers!

Twelve crows are sitting in a tree. A farmer comes along and shoots one. How many are left?

It takes ten minutes to hard-boil one egg. How long does it take to hard-boil four eggs?

Two children were bicycling down the road. The one in front said, "I'll be you a dollar that you can't beat me!" The other one said, "I won't bet you because I know that I can't win." How did he know that he couldn't win?

71 Noun-Verb Go-Round

I am partial to language arts games that require no materials. Here is another good one that stimulates creativity and provides practice in basic spelling and grammar.

The first player gives a two-word sentence made up of a noun and a verb, such as: "Stars shine." The next player must also state a two-word, noun-verb sentence, but the *first word* of his sentence must start with the *first two letters* of the last word in the previous statement. For example, after the first player says, "Stars *shine,*" the next player might say, "*Sh*oes *squeak.*" The next player might say, "*Sq*uirrels *cl*imb." The next could say, "*Cl*ouds burst." Play continues until someone misses.

72 Storm Warning

You are sure to remember this from your childhood. It remains one of the best thought-provoking activities.

A thunderstorm

The sound of thunder travels one mile in about five seconds. This is the usual method for calculating the distance of a storm center: As soon as you see lightning, start counting the seconds—until you hear thunder. (To count seconds, say one-one hundred, two one-hundred, etc.) Write down this number.

Divide the number by five. This tells you the approximate distance of the storm. If you counted to twenty-five, the storm is about five miles away.

Lightning and thunder actually occur at the same time. If this is so, then why don't you see and hear them at the same time?
(Light travels faster than sound.)

73 Flip Side

The ability to see something from a unique perspective is the hallmark of many creative people. This guessing game cultivates this ability and enhances deductive thinking skills.

The first player thinks of something to describe. It should be something that is generally thought of as beautiful or good. Here's the catch: The player must describe this thing *in negative terms*, giving three to five clues. The other player or players try to identify the object. To describe a chocolate chip cookie, a player might give these clues:

"It can make you fat."

"If it's too hot it can burn your tongue."

"If it sits too long, it gets hard."

"It has dark brown stuff in it."

Players get four chances to guess the object. The player who guesses correctly becomes the leader and describes a new object. If no one can guess correctly, the player gives the answer and tries again with a new object.

74 | What Am I?

I first encountered this game in a theater improvisation class, and it soon became a standard in my classroom and at home. It is especially valuable because it allows children to stretch their creative thinking in a nonverbal fashion. It is important to remember that a child can be creative, even if his or her written or oral language skills are slow to develop.

You need four or more people for this game. Players divide into teams of two or more. Each team decides to become a particular machine; each member of the team decides which part of the machine he or she will be. Be sure that players understand that each team is only *one* machine and each team member just part of that machine. Allow teams ten to fifteen minutes to practice.

Each team acts out the machine as the other teams tries to guess what it is. Sounds are allowed, but talking is discouraged. Simple props can be used, too.

Some of the machines that work well are: popcorn popper, microwave, television, radio, car, snowplow, refrigerator, typewriter, tow truck, clock, Ferris wheel, etc. This game is an excellent birthday party picker-upper.

75 Missing Word

This exercise increases vocabulary skills and creative thinking.

WHAT YOU AND YOUR CHILD DO

Make a few statements that give specific information but leave out a key word. For example: Tell what kind of a test you had today, but don't say *math*. Describe what you had for lunch today, but don't say *tuna*. Can another person figure out what you are trying to say? Take turns. It's not as easy as it sounds!

76 | Butter Batter

Making butter is a great way to introduce a child to the wonders of kitchen chemistry.

One jar with a tight-fitting lid
One cup of heavy cream

Pour the cream into the jar. Close the cover tightly and shake vigorously. Take turns, as you need to keep shaking for at least ten to fifteen minutes until a "lump" of butter will appear. It's delicious to serve your homemade butter on fresh, warm toast.

77 Morse, of Course

Use the international Morse code to cultivate memory and inference skills.

WHAT YOU NEED

A flashlight

An opaque piece of cloth; a small plastic dish; anything to cover the front of the flashlight

Paper and pencil

WHAT YOU AND YOUR CHILD DO

Make copies of the code as shown below. Take turns being receiver and sender. To signal a dash, uncover the flashlight for three to five seconds. For a dot, uncover the light for one second. If the flashing is difficult, you can just say the words, "dot" and "dash." Make sure that everyone has paper and pencil to keep track.

Morse code

A .-	H	O ---	V ...-
B -...	I ..	P .--.	W .--
C -.-.	J .---	Q --.-	X -..-
D -..	K -.-	R .-.	Y -.--
E .	L .-..	S ...	Z --..
F ..-.	M --	T -	? ..--..
G --.	N -.	U ..-	Period .-.-.-

78 | In and Out of Character

WHAT YOU AND YOUR CHILD DO

The following exercise combines dramatic play with creative problem-solving. It is also fun for the entire family.

Think of a situation in which a character must solve a problem. For example: If Peter Pan tripped and fell into a very deep, dark pit, how would he escape? Act out this situation.

Now act out the same situation with a different character. (How would Cinderella get out of the pit?) Use characters from fairy tales, literature, and TV and movies.

Here are some suggested dilemmas just to get you started. Be adventurous. Place a fairy tale character in a contemporary setting and vice versa.

As you cross the bridge, you hear the mean troll.

You are locked out of your castle.

You ran out of toothpaste.

Your spaceship is out of fuel.

You forgot to do your homework.

You see a tornado approaching.

If it's necessary, prompt each player to stay in character! "Is that how Peter Pan would talk? How would he walk?" After a few rounds, players should get the hang of it.

Yes, We Have No Bananas

My students love this code, sometimes called the supermarket code. I love it because it enhances basic vocabulary skills and creative thinking.

Pencil and paper

To write a message in supermarket code, use numbers and letters in this way:

The first letter in ham is H, so the first letter in the message is also H. The fifth letter in apples is E, so the next letter in the message is E. As you go on in this way, you will discover that the message is "HELLO."

Write a message in this code. Give your partner the shopping list, and the first two letters of your message. Can he or she figure out what the code is? Explain the code and send messages to each other.

Will the Real Gibbles Please Stand Up . . .

Attribute puzzles are those in which you use inductive and deductive reasoning to figure out what attributes are shared by a certain group. Here are some easy ones to start. Try them with your child. The answers are in the back of the book, but don't peek.

Solve these puzzles.

1.

All of these are Gibbles.

None of these are Gibbles.

Which of these are Gibbles?

2.

All of these are Bleeples.

None of these are Bleeples.

Which of these are Bleeples?

Now make up some of your own attribute puzzles.

81 | Through the Looking Glass

A magnifying glass could be your child's first look at the possibilities of the world of science. It's worth your while to purchase a strong, sturdy magnifying glass from a school supply or hobby store.

Magnifying glass
Paper
Pencil, markers, or crayons

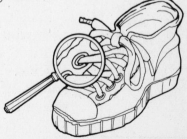

Start by looking at ordinary items (shoes, rocks, books, clothes, etc.) with a magnifying glass. Describe each object. Then describe how each object appears when viewed through the glass.

Fold a piece of paper in half. On one side draw a picture of an object as it appears when you look at it with your eyes. On the other side draw a picture of what you see as you view it through the magnifying glass. Does the magnifying glass actually change the size of something or does it just change the way we see it?

If you are lucky enough to have two magnifying glasses, experiment by holding the two lenses together and looking through them. This is the way a microscope works.

82 Daffynitions

This game strengthens skills of inference and creativity—and can become very funny!

A dictionary
Pencil and paper

The first player uses the dictionary to locate a word that the other players probably do not know. Read the word aloud. Give the other players two to five minutes to invent a definition for the word. They can say it, write it, or draw a picture of it.

There are two ways to play this game. Players can try to infer the real meaning of the word, or they can piece the syllables together to create a funny definition.

Examples of both methods are below.

"outlandish"—far from land

"outlandish"—a dish that sits out on the land, good for picnics

Don't forget to read the real definition when you're done!

83 North by Northwest

Most adults and children are threatened by scientific instruments because they never use them. Start your child out with a sturdy, practical piece of scientific technology—a compass.

WHAT YOU NEED

One compass

Paper and pencil

A wrapped prize or treat for the end of a treasure hunt

TREASURE MAP

• WALK NORTH 3 STEPS
• WALK EAST 2 STEPS
• WALK SOUTH 5 STEPS
• FIND TREASURE!

WHAT YOU AND YOUR CHILD DO

Hide the treasure. Use the compass to map out a route to the treasure. Start out with no more than three directions: Walk north three steps. Walk east two steps. Walk south five steps. Write down the directions.

Show your child exactly where to start. Using the compass, he or she must follow your directions to find the prize. Take turns mapping a route and searching for the treasure.

84 Riddle Factory

As their language skills mature, children begin to discover and enjoy riddles. Riddles are treasure chests of word plays and puns, tied together with large doses of creative thinking. Making up riddles is a challenging way to sharpen skills in all those areas. Here are some suggestions for your own riddle factory.

WHAT YOU NEED

Pencil and paper

WHAT YOU AND YOUR CHILD DO

Write down the name of an object and its characteristics. Example:

ladder: goes up and down; reaches high places; you climb it.

Try to combine some of the characteristics to make a riddle. The key here is to look for characteristics that are opposite or paradoxical. For example: "What goes up and down, but stays in the same place?" A ladder.

Another way to create a riddle is to use homonym pairs. Homonyms are words that sound the same, but are spelled differently. Pail and pale are homonyms. Here's one: Why is a ghost like a small bucket? Because they're both a little pale/pail. How is the tailor different from the liar? One is not who he seems; and one is what he seams!

STEAK   STAKE

MAIL

MALE

Here are some homonyms to get you going:

bear—bare	flee—flea	plain—plane
brake—break	foul—fowl	steak—stake
deer—dear	heal—heel	steel—steal
dough—doe	male—mail	tale—tail
fare—fair	meet—meat	wear—where

Using these or other homonyms, you can write riddles by filling in the blanks: "How is a _____ like a _____ ?" or "How is a _____ different from a _____ ?"

85 Something in the Way It Moves

Here is a simple demonstration and experiment that allows a child to discover a basic scientific concept: Sound is caused by vibration. Don't miss this easy opportunity for hands-on discovery.

WHAT YOU NEED

Two pot lids

Rubber bands

Drums or any other percussion instruments (optional)

Sound is made when something *moves*. Bang two lids together and listen to the sound. Look at the lids. Are they moving? Bang them together again and quickly put your hand on one. What happens? Strum a rubber band. Listen and look! What happens when you stop the rubber band?

Most children are amazed by this revelation and are anxious to experiment further. Put your hand on your throat when you talk or sing. What is moving? Tap water glasses filled with various levels of water. What is moving? What other ways can you find to demonstrate the concept that sound is made by movement?

86 Cool Cartoons

Have you ever clipped out a cartoon because it so perfectly expressed an experience you wanted to share? Encourage your child to find and display cartoons. It will help develop skills of symbolic transformation and creativity—and it's a lot of fun besides!

Scissors
Cartoons from newspapers, magazines, etc.
Tape or kitchen magnet

Cut out any cartoon that expresses an idea you want to share. Encourage your child to do the same. Don't forget political cartoons or cartoons found in different sections of the paper, such as the business section.

The refrigerator is usually a favorite repository for family notices, papers, and all items of interest. Start a "cool cartoon corner" on your refrigerator. Whenever a new cartoon appears, discuss it. Ask: "Do you get it? Do you think it's funny? True? Why or why not?"

This is an excellent way for family members to express peeves or wishes that are difficult to confront directly. Reactions to cartoons often reveal much about feelings.

87 | Hot Ice

We usually wear dark-colored clothes in the winter and light colors in the summer. This experiment is an impressive demonstration of the way science is part of what we do every day.

WHAT YOU NEED

Several ice cubes
One piece of white cloth
One piece of black or dark-colored cloth
Sunlight or a bright lamp

WHAT YOU AND YOUR CHILD DO

Experimenting with ice cubes can help us learn about the way dark and light colors absorb heat. When do we usually wear white and light colors? When do we wear darker colors? This experiment should show us the reasons behind these choices.

Wrap one ice cube in the white cloth. Wrap another in the dark cloth. Place both in a sunny location, or under a bright lamp. Which one will melt faster? Why?

A variation of this activity is to cut out two circles exactly the same size. Color one yellow and one black. Paste them on a piece of paper and tack it to a wall. Stand across the room and look at the circles. Does one look bigger? Why?

Celebrity Celebrations

Everyone loves a party. Here's a way to transform any party into a learning experience for the whole family.

Reference books with information about birthday celebrants
Appropriate decorations (optional)

Once a month celebrate the birthday of a person who has made an important contribution to civilization. Research and plan appropriate activities. Make a special meal; share information about the person; sing "Happy Birthday." Play a composer's music, share an artist's work, read from a writer's books, etc.

This activity can do more than impart information. It presents the opportunity for you to demonstrate positive values and judgment. The people you honor will not necessarily be *famous*. Use newspapers and magazines to learn about and salute a living, local hero, such as a woman who raised money for a worthy cause or a man who spoke out in support of an issue you consider worthwhile.

89 What's in a Symbol?

We are surrounded by symbols: street signs, markings on a car's controls, maps, trademarks, flags, and so on. Even preschoolers enjoy decoding messages that mean "no smoking" or "danger." Take advantage of the wealth of symbols in your environment.

WHAT YOU NEED

Paper
Pencil and markers

WHAT YOU AND YOUR CHILD DO

Point out various symbols and discuss why symbols might be used instead of words. Design a few of your own symbols. Here are some suggestions. Create a symbol that means:

> No kid sisters (brothers) allowed
> Quiet: Study Time
> No sardines (or some other disliked food . . .)
> Do not get this wet
> Funny
> Sad
> Sorry

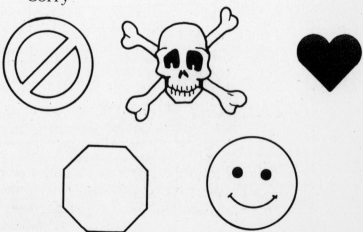

My Grand Old Flag

Designing a personal emblem reinforces encoding skills. It can also provide an opportunity to build self-esteem.

WHAT YOU NEED

Reference books
White tissue paper or tracing paper
Pencil
Colored paper
Scissors
Glue
Crayons or markers

WHAT YOU AND YOUR CHILD DO

Use an encyclopedia or other reference books to find flags for various countries. Find out what the colors and various symbols mean and share this information with your child. Suggest making an individual or family flag.

Make a list of your best attributes: likes mysteries, loves outdoors, loves to take vacations, good sense of humor, honest, sensitive, good friend.

Narrow down the list and next to each attribute draw a symbol.

Loves to
take vacations

Loves
outdoors

Good friend

Good sense
of humor

Look at the new list and find a way to combine the symbols into a flag design. You can leave out one or more of the symbols, or you can use them all.

91

Popcorn Science

I never knew what made popcorn pop until I tried this experiment with my children. Once you provide some of the basic information, give your child a chance to express his or her own hypothesis. Close supervision is required for this activity.

WHAT YOU NEED

Two bags of microwave popcorn
Microwave
Baking sheet
Oven

WHAT YOU AND YOUR CHILD DO

What is a kernel of corn? It is a seed, and all seeds have some water inside to nourish them until they are ready to grow. This little bit of water is what makes popcorn pop! When the kernel is heated *quickly* the water changes into gas. This gas keeps expanding until the kernel explodes.

Heat the oven to 200 degrees. Open one bag of microwave popcorn and spread the kernels out in a single layer on the baking sheet. Bake the corn for an hour and a half. What do you think will happen to this popcorn?

After you have removed the popcorn from the oven, make the other bag of microwave popcorn according to the directions given on the package. Which method created the most popcorn? Which method made the biggest kernels? Why? What did the long, slow baking in the oven do to the water inside the popcorn kernels?

Here are a few follow-up questions: What would happen if you heated the popcorn in the oven for an even longer time? Why is it important that popcorn be fresh?

92 Mindreader

WHAT YOU AND YOUR CHILD DO

Any guessing game, such as the classic "Twenty Questions" is always worth your time. Here is one that reinforces basic math and deductive reasoning skills.

The first player thinks of a number and tells the other players how many digits are in the number. Start with two-digit numbers. The other players try to guess the number. After each guess, the leader tells each player:

if he or she guessed any numbers correctly

if any of the numbers were both correct and *in the right place*

For example, if the hidden number is 25, and a player guesses 15, that player must be told that one number is correct and is also in the right place. The player should *not* be told *which* of his digits is the correct one!

93 The Price Is Right

Estimation is a math skill that is receiving serious attention. In our fast-paced world there are many instances in which a close guess serves just as well as the perfect answer. People who master this skill can make math problem-solving much easier.

WHAT YOU NEED

Trip to the grocery store for ten to twenty items

WHAT YOU AND YOUR CHILD DO

As you do the marketing, read the price of each item aloud. Ask your child to keep an estimated running total of what you are spending. No calculators or paper allowed! If your child comes close to the actual total, give him or her a reward! As you improve, expand the activity to include a longer list of items.

94 Correspondence Code

This activity combines two sure-fire winners: puzzles and secret messages. It builds visual logic and deductive reasoning skills at the same time

WHAT YOU NEED

Old magazines, comics, or coloring books
Construction paper
Glue
Scissors
Markers
Envelopes
Stamps

WHAT YOU AND YOUR CHILD DO

Paste a picture from a magazine, comic, or coloring book onto a piece of construction paper. Write a message on the back of the construction paper, and then draw a design of geometric puzzle shapes on the same side of the sheet. Carefully cut apart the shapes. Send the puzzle pieces to a friend or give them to a family member. He or she puts the puzzle picture together, tapes it with clear tape, and turns it over to read the secret message.

Do you have any snapshots that are "outtakes"—not good enough to keep in the family album? These disposable photos make wonderful correspondence code cards. Write a message on the back of a photo and cut it into puzzle pieces. The recipient can tape it back together and turn it over to read the secret message.

95 Dillar, Dollar

Most children are fascinated with money. Take advantage of this interest and stretch numerical problem-solving skills. The solution to this classic puzzler is at the end of this book, but resist the temptation to look now.

WHAT YOU NEED

Fifty pennies
Ten nickels
Four dimes
Two quarters

WHAT YOU AND YOUR CHILD DO

Challenge your child to make $1.00 in change—using *exactly* fifty coins.

96 Math Magic

This math puzzle stimulates a variety of higher level thinking skills, including inference and deduction.

WHAT YOU NEED

Paper and pencil

Copy the following diagram:

Fill in the boxes so that the sum of each side adds up to 15. You can use only the numbers 1, 2, 3, 4, 5, 6, 7, and 8, and you can use each number only *once*.

Hint: write down all the combinations of three numbers that can add up to 15.

This kind of math puzzle is known as a *magic square*. Look for more in the library.

97 Talk Is Not Always Cheap

Children of all ages love this activity. It is wonderful for developing creative problem-solving skills as well as basic addition review.

Paper and pencil
A dictionary

GAYLE = 50¢
BRIAN = 44¢

G = 7¢
A = 1¢

Assign each letter of the alphabet a value: A = 1, B = 2, etc. Write out this cents-alphabet code. Use this code to find words that add up to exactly one dollar (or pretty close).

My students love using this code for a variety of money-alphabet activities. In addition to this one above, they would:

> find the numerical value of their names
>
> find the "most expensive" name in the room
>
> find the "cheapest" name
>
> compare the numerical value in the names of toys to the retail prices

98 Lucky Thirteen

This is my favorite kind of thinking game. It involves manipulation, seems easier than it is, and forces you to think *before* you act.

Thirteen objects

Spread the objects on the table. The first player removes one or two objects from the table. Each player takes turns removing objects, one or two at a time. Here is the catch: The loser is the one who removes the *last* object!

99 Crazy Libs

This is a homemade version of the commercial word game in which you substitute parts of speech with hilarious results. It has long been an educational favorite because it teaches basic vocabulary and syntax with a game that adults like as well as children.

WHAT YOU NEED

Paper and pencil

WHAT YOU AND YOUR CHILD DO

Start by creating a simple story in which you leave out several key parts of speech:

You may want to begin by making a list of nouns, verbs, and adjectives. As your child becomes more familiar with the parts of speech, you can write more complex stories. You can also use old comic books and magazines as samples. Use a bottle of typewriter correction fluid to "white out" the key words and write in your own.

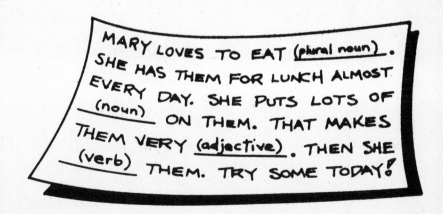

MARY LOVES TO EAT (plural noun). SHE HAS THEM FOR LUNCH ALMOST EVERY DAY. SHE PUTS LOTS OF (noun) ON THEM. THAT MAKES THEM VERY (adjective). THEN SHE (verb) THEM. TRY SOME TODAY!

100 | City Seedlings

Even confirmed city dwellers probably have everything they need to grow these seedlings. When experimenting with growing things, it is important to remember to learn from your mistakes. If your seedlings don't grow, try to figure out what might have gone wrong and try again.

WHAT YOU NEED

Seeds from grapefruits, lemons, or oranges
Potting soil
Planting containers (You can use plastic food storage bowls. Just cut a few drainage holes in the bottom.)
Water

WHAT YOU AND YOUR CHILD DO

Soak the seeds in water overnight. Plant them about an inch deep in the soil. Place your plant in a sunny spot and keep the soil moist. If all goes well, your seedlings will sprout leaves and a flower.

While waiting for your seedlings to grow, research flowering fruit trees. Do all fruit trees have flowers? Why? Find pictures of various fruit flowers. What will your flowers look like?

101 | Add 'Em Up

A math teacher told me about this game. It is very popular with her students, and I can see why. This is another game that includes manipulation and strategy.

5	5	5	5	5
4	4	4	4	4
3	3	3	3	3
2	2	2	2	2
1	1	1	1	1

WHAT YOU AND YOUR CHILD DO

Copy this onto the poster board.

One player selects a target number—any number between 20 and 55—and writes it down. The first player uses a marker to cover one number on the board and calls out this number.

The next player covers one more number, adds his or her number to the last one covered and calls out the sum. (It's a good idea for one player to act as recorder and record each new sum.)

Play continues with each player covering a new number, adding it to the previous sum and calling out the new sum. Use each square only once. The first player to reach the target number is the winner. He must reach it *exactly*.

Answers

9: IF THE SOCK FITS . . .
You would need to take out seven socks

21: LISTEN, MY CHILDREN
The owner has blond hair if *you* do! Remember that you were told to pretend that *you* were the owner of the gift shop.

66: NO REPEATS
QH	JS	AD	KC
AC	KD	QS	JH
KS	AH	JC	QD
JD	QC	KH	AS

70: MORE TRICKY THINKING
A) None are left. The others are frightened by the shot and fly away.
B) Ten minutes.
C) They are on a bicycle built for two.

80: GIBBLES
1. A and C are Gibbles
2. B is a Bleeple.

95: DILLAR, DOLLAR
45 pennies, one quarter, two dimes, two nickels or
40 pennies, two dimes, eight nickels

96: MATH MAGIC
8 - 1 - 6
4   2
3 - 5 - 7